Snowman

C R A F T S

Sheila A. Bergner

Phyllis Dunstan

Trena Hegdahl

Charlene Messerle

Carol Neu

Publications International, Ltd.

Sheila A. Bergner is a woodworker, painter, and craft pattern designer. She is a member of the Society of Decorative Painters and coeditor of the *Scroll Saw News*. Shelia's designs have been published in the magazines *Craftworks, Creative Woodworks,* and *Crafts.*

Phyllis Dunstan is an artist and craft designer who has had her designs published in various magazines and books. Her list of publications includes *Incredibly Awesome Crafts for Kids* and *Creative Activity Kit: Flying Power,* as well as contributions to the magazines *Sunset* and *Redbook.* Phyllis also frequently teaches classes and gives craft demonstrations.

Trena Hegdahl is the owner of Mine & Yours, a pattern and design company, where she frequently writes and designs for magazines and develops new products for manufacturers. She has made numerous television appearances, and her work has appeared in a variety of books, including *Christmas Crafts* and *Creative Activity Kit: Friendship Fun.*

Charlene Messerle is a floral designer who has been published in magazines, books, and videos. Her work has been featured in magazines such as *Better Homes and Gardens, Crafts 'n Things,* and *Christmas Crafts,* and the book *Garden Crafts.* Charlene is a member of the Society of Craft Designers.

Carol Neu is a freelance artist who has been involved in decorative painting for many years. She has been published in many magazines and books, including *Treasury of Holiday Crafts, Stocking Stuffer Fun,* and *Decorative Wood Crafts.*

Photography: Peter Dean Ross/Peter Dean Ross Photographs; Jennifer Marx

Stylist: Lisa Wright

Models: Theresa Lesniak and Courtney Reubin/Royal Model Management

Louis Weber, CEO
Publications International, Ltd.
7373 North Cicero Avenue
Lincolnwood, Illinois 60712

Manufactured in China.

8 7 6 5 4 3 2 1

ISBN: 1-4127-1069-3

Contents

Page 10

Page 14

Page 17

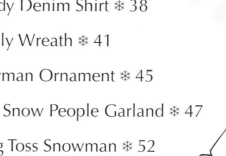

Page 56

KIDS' KORNER

Page 60

Snowman Crafting

WINTERS CAN BE THE WARMEST and happiest time of the year for many people—children and adults alike! Not only do special holidays fall during the winter, but life seems to slow down a bit during those cold months. This is also the time when creating decorations and presents is most fun and fulfilling—and most appreciated by those receiving lovingly made gifts. Remember, things made by hand come from the heart.

The projects in this book include a wide variety of techniques and methods. Take a moment to look through the pages. You'll find everything from decorative wood painting to sewing. Crafting is a wonderful way to escape the crowded shopping malls and the mad race to find that "perfect" gift. Now you'll be able to make something wonderful for just about everyone on your gift list right at home! In *Snowman Crafts,* you will find many crafts that take a day or less to create. Each project has complete step-by-step instructions and photos to help make everything easy to understand and fun to do.

We hope you enjoy creating these projects. They are for all skill levels and interests. You'll find that many of the projects use basic items you already have around your home. Once you begin, you'll see that crafting is a satisfying and relaxing way to spend your time.

What You'll Find

A WORD ABOUT GLUE

Glue can be a sticky subject when you don't use the right one for the job. There are many different glues on the craft market today, each formulated for a different crafting purpose. The following are ones you should be familiar with:

White glue: This may be used as an all-purpose glue—it dries clear and flexible. It is often referred to as craft glue or tacky glue. Tacky on contact, it allows you to put two items together without a lot of set-up time required. Use it for most projects, especially ones involving wood, plastics, some fabrics, and cardboard.

Thin-bodied glues: Use these glues when your project requires a smooth, thin layer of glue. Thin-bodied glues work well on some fabrics and papers.

Fabric glue: This type of glue is made to bond with fabric fibers and withstand repeated washing. Use this glue for attaching rhinestones and/or other charms to fabric projects. Some glues require heat-setting. Check the bottle for complete instructions.

Hot-melt glue: Formed into cylindrical sticks, this glue is inserted into a hot-temperature glue gun and heated to a liquid state. Depending on the type of glue gun used, the glue is forced out through the gun's nozzle by either pushing on the end of the glue stick or squeezing a trigger. Use clear glue sticks for projects using wood, fabrics, most plastics, ceramics, and cardboard. When using any glue gun, be careful of the nozzle and the freshly applied glue—it is very hot! Apply glue to the piece being attached. Work with small areas so the glue doesn't set before the object is pressed into place.

Low-melt glue: This is similar to hot-melt glue in that it is formed into sticks and requires a glue gun to be used. Low-melt glue is used for projects that would be damaged by heat, such as foam, balloons, and metallic ribbons. Low-melt glue sticks are oval-shaped and can only be used in a low-temperature glue gun.

GENERAL PATTERN INSTRUCTIONS

When a project's instructions tell you to cut out a shape according to the pattern, trace the pattern from the book onto tracing paper, using a pencil. If the pattern has an arrow with the word *FOLD* next to a line, it is a half pattern. Fold a sheet of tracing paper in half, and open up the paper. Place the fold line of the tracing paper exactly on top of the fold line of the pattern, and trace the pattern with a pencil. Then refold and cut along the line, going through both layers. Open the paper for the full pattern.

Some of the patterns in this book are printed smaller than actual size. Enlarge them on a photocopier before using them, copying the pattern at the percentage indicated near the pattern.

CRAFTING WITH KIDS

There are special projects in this book made especially for kids to craft. But they will still need your help and guidance, depending on their age and abilities. You are the best judge of this. Make sure your child reads through the instructions carefully before deciding whether the project requires adult supervision. If the child has never used a glue gun, explain that both the nozzle and freshly applied glue are hot. Have a glass of water nearby just in case warm fingers need cooling. Also, if kids will be painting with acrylic paints, have them wear an apron, because after the paint dries, it is permanent. If paint does get on clothes, wash them with soap and warm water immediately.

WEARABLES

Prewash fabrics, but don't use any fabric softeners, which prevent adhesives and paint from bonding with the fibers. Press out wrinkles. After you're done with your project, hand or machine wash in lukewarm water—NOT COLD—on delicate/knit cycle. Tumble dry on low for a few minutes to remove wrinkles, then remove and lay flat to dry. Do **not** use delicate care wash products; use regular laundry detergent.

SEWING

The excitement of making your own holiday crafts sometimes gets in the way of your preparation. Before plunging into your chosen project, check to make sure you have all the materials needed. Being prepared will make your sewing easier and more fun. Most of the items you need will probably be on hand already.

Fusible (or adhesive) webbing: A lightweight fusible iron-on webbing is time-saving and easy to use. The webbing is placed paper side up on the wrong side of the material. Place iron on paper side of webbing, and press for one to three seconds. Allow fabric to cool. Designs can then be drawn or traced onto the paper side and cut out. Remove the paper, place the material right side up in desired position on project, and iron for three to five seconds.

Ironing board and steam iron: Sometimes you do more sewing with the iron than you do with the sewing machine. Be sure your ironing board is well padded and has a clean covering. Keeping your fabrics, seams, and hems pressed cuts down on stitches and valuable time. A steam or dry iron is best. It is important to press your fabric to achieve a professional look. The iron is also used to adhere the fusible interfacing. Keep the bottom of your iron clean and free of any substance that could mark your fabric. The steam iron may be used directly on most fabrics with no shine. Test a small piece of the fabric first. If it causes a shine on the right side, try ironing on the wrong side of the fabric.

Sewing machine: Neat, even stitches are achieved in a few minutes with a sewing machine, and it helps you complete your project with ease. If desired, you can machine sew a zigzag stitch around the ironed-on pieces to secure the edges.

Scissors: You will need two styles. One kind is about eight to ten inches long with bent handles for cutting fabric. This style of scissors allows you to cut through the fabric while it lays flat. These shears should be sharp and used only for fabric. The second style of scissors is smaller, about six inches, with sharp points. You will need this style for smaller projects and close areas.

Straight pins: Nonrusting dressmaker pins are best to use. They will not leave rust marks on your fabric if they come in contact with dampness or glue. And dressmaker's pins have very sharp points for easy insertion.

Tape measure: This should be plastic coated so that it will not stretch and can be wiped off if it comes in contact with paint or glue.

Thread: Have mercerized sewing thread in the colors needed for each project you have chosen. Proper shade and strength (about 50 weight) of thread avoids having the stitching show more than is necessary and will give the item a more finished look.

Work surface: Your sewing surface should be a comfortable height for sitting and roomy enough to lay out your projects. Keep it clean and free of other crafting materials that could accidently spill or soil your fabric.

WOODWORKING

A band saw and a scroll saw are very handy, easy-to-use tools for the home workshop. They may be easily operated by a man, woman, or even an older teen with adult supervision.

Respect your saw—Safety First! Before you begin, read your instruction manual. And always keep in mind these simple safety hints when using any saw:

- Keep your work area clean and uncluttered.
- Don't use saw in damp or wet locations.
- Keep your work area well lit.
- Do not force saw through items it is not designed for.
- Wear proper clothing—nothing loose or baggy.
- Wear safety goggles.
- Never leave saw unattended.

DECORATIVE WOOD PAINTING

Decorative painting has been handed down from generation to generation. It's an art form that was developed by untrained artists, and no artistic talent or drawing skills are necessary. All you need is the desire to create useful and beautiful items to decorate your home.

Once you start painting arts and craft projects, you'll be hooked. Let the dishes and dusting wait, and indulge yourself by experiencing the pleasure of painting. You will surprise even yourself with what you can make, as you create decorative pieces for your home. You will also impress your friends while indulging in the fun of making gifts for friends and loved ones.

There are a large variety of styles and finishes to choose from in the following pages. Many can be completed in only a couple hours. These pages will walk you through some common techniques. Have fun creating all of the decoratively painted pieces ahead.

SUPPLIES

PAINTS

There are a wide variety of paint brands to choose from. Acrylic paints are available at your local arts and crafts stores in a wide variety of brands. Mix and match your favorite colors to paint the projects in this book. These projects will work with any acrylic paint brands.

Acrylic paint dries in minutes and allows projects to be completed in no time at all. Clean hands and brushes with soap and water.

Some projects may require a medium that is not acrylic or water based. These require mineral spirits to clean up. Always check the manufacturer's label before working with a product so you have the proper supplies available.

FINISHES

Choose from a wide variety of types and brands of varnishes to protect your finished project. Varnish is available in both spray and brush-on.

Brush-on water-base varnishes dry in minutes and clean up with soap and water. Use over any acrylic paints. Don't use over paints or mediums requiring mineral spirits to clean up.

Spray varnishes can be used over any type of paint or medium. For projects with a pure white surface, choose a nonyellowing varnish. The slight yellowing of some varnishes can actually enhance certain projects for a richer look. Varnishes are available in matte, satin, or gloss finishes. Choose the shine you prefer.

BRUSHES

Foam (sponge) brushes work well to seal, base coat, and varnish wood. Clean foam brushes with soap and water when using acrylic paints and mediums. For paints or mediums that require mineral spirits to clean up, you will have to throw the disposable brush away.

Synthetic brushes work well with acrylic paints for details and designs. Use a liner brush for thin lines and details. A script brush is needed for extra long lines. Round brushes fill in round areas, stroke work, and broad lines. An angle brush is used to fill in large areas, float, or side-load color. A large flat brush is used to apply basecoat and varnish. A small flat brush is for stroke work and base coating small areas.

Specialty brushes, including a stencil brush and a fabric round scrubber, can be used for stencil painting and stippling. The Kemper tool or an old toothbrush can be used to spatter paint.

WOOD PREPARATION

Properly preparing your wood piece can make all the difference in the outcome. Having a smooth surface to work on will allow you to complete the project quickly and easily. Once the wood is prepared, you are ready to proceed with a base coat, stain, or finish, according to the project instructions. Some finishes, such as crackling, will recommend not sealing the wood. Always read instructions completely before starting.

Supplies you will need to prepare the wood: sandpaper (#200) for removing roughness; tack cloth, which is a sticky resin-treated cheese cloth, to remove dust after sanding; a wood sealer to seal wood and prevent warping; and a foam or 1-inch flat brush to apply sealer.

Note: Wood with knot holes requires a special sealer to prevent sap from later bleeding through the paint. Check the manufacturer's label for proper usage.

1. Choose a clear wood sealer for transparent finishes. Any rough edges should be presanded using #200 sandpaper. Wipe wood clean with a tack cloth. Use a foam or large flat brush to apply sealer. Allow sealer to dry completely. You can use a hair dryer to speed drying time, if desired.

2. Once the wood has been sealed and is dry, the grain will raise slightly. Sand with #200 sandpaper to smooth surface. Rub your hand across the surface to check for any missed rough spots. Wipe surface with a tack cloth to remove dust particles.

TRANSFERRING DESIGNS

You don't have to know anything about drawing to transfer a design. The designs in this book can be transferred directly onto the project surface. Simply follow the instructions for a fast and easy transformation.

Transfer supplies: Transparent tracing paper, pencil or fine marker, scissors, tape, transfer paper (carbon or graphite), and stylus.

1. Place transparent tracing paper over the design you want to copy. Trace the design lines with a pencil or fine marker. Trace only the lines you absolutely need to complete the project. The transparent paper allows you to position the pattern on the wood project. Cut excess paper to whatever shape or size is easiest to work with. Tape a few edges down to hold the pattern in place.

2. Place a piece of transfer paper, carbon side down, between the wood and the pattern. Choose a color that will easily show on your project. Use a stylus or pencil to trace over the design lines. Lift a corner of the pattern to make sure the design is transferring properly.

BASIC PAINTING TECHNIQUES

THIN LINES

1. Thin paint with 50 percent water for a fluid consistency that flows easily off the brush. It should be about ink consistency.

2. Use a liner brush for short lines and tiny details or a script brush for long lines. Dip brush into thinned paint. Wipe excess on palette.

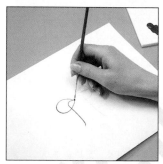

3. Hold brush upright with handle pointing to the ceiling. Use your little finger as a balance when painting. Don't apply pressure for extra thin lines.

FLOATING COLOR

This technique is also called side-loading. It is used to shade or highlight the edge of an object. Floated color is a gradual blend of color to water.

1. Moisten an angle brush with water. Blot excess water from brush, setting bristles on paper towel until shine of water disappears.

2. Dip the long corner of angle brush into paint. Load paint sparingly. Carefully stroke brush on palette until color blends halfway across the brush. If the paint blends all the way to short side, clean and load again. For a wider band of color, dilute paint first with 50 percent water.

3. Hold the brush at a 45-degree angle, and use a light touch to apply color to designated area.

STIPPLING

Create a textured look on an area. This technique is great for foliage, snow, and background effects.

1. Use undiluted paint for heavy texture or dilute with 50 to 80 percent water for a soft, faint texture. Dip a fabric scrubber, stencil brush, or old scruffy brush into paint. Dab excess paint on paper towel.

2. Hold brush upright, and pounce tip of brush repeatedly in area until desired texture is reached. For a light and airy look, don't fill area in completely; allow some of the background to show through.

SPATTERING

Little dots of paint are sprinkled on the surface, which is great for creating snow, making an aged fly spec look, or just adding fun colors to a finish. Always test spattering on paper first.

1. Thin paint with 50 to 80 percent water. Use an old toothbrush and palette knife or a Kemper tool. Dip brush into thinned paint. Lots of paint on the brush will create large dots. As paint runs out, dots become finer.

2. With a toothbrush, drag your thumb or palette knife across the top of the bristles causing them to bend. As you release, the bristles spring forward, spattering the paint onto the surface.

ALTERNATIVES

1. A Kemper tool is like a tiny baby bottle washer with a wire that bends the bristles as you twist the handle. To use, hold the brush over the object to be spattered and twist the handle.

2. Or, hold a large flat brush vertically in one hand over the surface. Hold the handle of another brush under it horizontally. Tap handle against handle.

DOTS

Perfect round dots can be made with any round implement. The size of the implement determines the size of the dot. You can use the wooden end of a paintbrush, a stylus tip, a pencil tip, or the eraser end of a pencil (with an unused eraser).

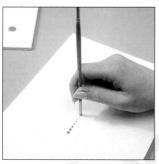

1. Use undiluted paint for thick dots or dilute paint with 50 percent water for smooth dots. Dip the tip into paint and then onto the surface. For uniform dots, you must redip in paint for each dot. For graduated dots, continue dotting with same paint load. Clean tip on paper towel after each group and reload.

2. To create hearts, place two dots of the same size next to each other. Then drag paint from each dot down to meet in bottom of heart.

BOWS AND RIBBONS

There are many ways to make bows, and the more you make, the easier it becomes. Cutting the ribbon ends at an angle lends a more polished appearance to the finished product.

MAKING A MULTILOOP BOW

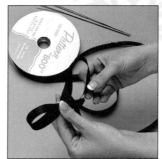

1. Unroll several yards from a bolt of ribbon. Form loops from the ribbon with your dominant hand. Pinch the center of the loops with the thumb and forefinger of your other hand as you work.

2. Continue to add loops to your bow. Keep pinching the bow's center with your thumb and forefinger. After you have all the loops you desire, trim excess ribbon from the bolt. If you want a streamer, leave the ribbon longer before cutting.

3. Place a length of wire around the center of the ribbon. Twist the wire securely around the bow's center to eliminate loop slippage. Attach the bow with the wire. You may also trim the wire and glue the bow in place.

Note: When using heavier ribbon, use a chenille stem to secure the bow. The tiny hairs on the stem will hold the bow securely. For tiny, delicate bows, use thin cloth-covered wire. It eliminates slipping and is so tiny that it disappears into the bow loops.

SANDY THE SNOWY
Stack Boxes

This captivating cutie can hold candy or small surprises for your visitors, or it will look just charming on a table—keeping you company all winter long!

What You'll Need

Paintbrushes: sponge, liner, ½-inch flat

Acrylic paint: white, turquoise, purple, orange, yellow, fuchsia, black

3 hatboxes: 2×3½ inches, 5×2½ inches, 3×5½ inches

1½-inch wood knob with flat bottom

½-inch wood button

Pencil

Glue gun, glue sticks

5 buttons, ⅝ inch each: 2 fuchsia, 2 green, 1 yellow

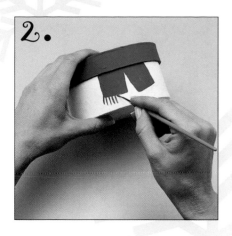

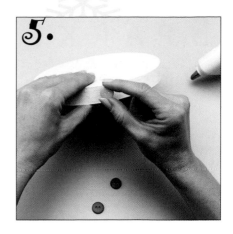

1. With the sponge brush, paint all hatboxes and lids white. Let dry. Paint medium lid turquoise. Paint small lid and wood knob purple. Paint ½-inch button orange. Let lids and button dry. If needed, apply another coat of paint after the first dries.

2. With pencil, lightly draw scarf on medium hatbox. Paint scarf turquoise. Let dry. (Paint another coat if needed.) With liner brush, paint turquoise fringe on bottom edge of scarf. Let dry.

3. With yellow paint and paintbrush end, make dots on the scarf and medium lid.

4. Glue orange button to center of small hatbox for nose. With flat brush, paint cheeks using fuchsia paint. Dot eyes and mouth with black paint and paint-brush end.

5. Glue wood knob to center top of small lid. Glue buttons to center front of medium hatbox, large lid, and large hatbox.

SPARKLING AND FROSTY
Stunning Shirt

Who knew a snowman could be so glamorous?
This rhinestone shirt will catch
everyone's eye!

What You'll Need

Tracing paper

Pencil

Pins

Black long-sleeve T-shirt

White dressmaker's carbon

Waxed paper

Jewelry glue

Tweezers

56 to 60 clear crystal
rhinestones, 4mm each

15 to 20 brown bugle beads

2 clear crystal seed beads

1 orange bugle bead

1. Enlarge and trace or photocopy pattern below. Center and pin pattern to front of T-shirt.

2. Slip dressmaker's carbon under pattern, with carbon side touching shirt. With the pencil, transfer dots and dashes from pattern to shirt.

3. Squeeze a small amount of glue onto waxed paper. Use tweezers to pick up a rhinestone and dip bottom into glue. Position rhinestone on T-shirt. Press in place with your finger. Repeat with remaining rhinestones.

4. Proceed in same manner to glue brown bugle beads in place for arms.

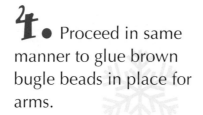

5. Glue 2 seed beads in place for eyes, and glue on orange bugle bead for nose. Let dry overnight before wearing. (Check glue package directions for washing instructions.)

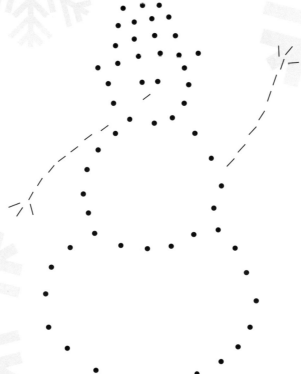

Enlarge pattern 150%.

MARVELOUS
Mantel Plate

This snowman plate will brighten any fireplace, shelf, or table in your home!

What You'll Need

Wood plate

Medium grade sandpaper

Tack cloth

Acrylic paint: deep midnight blue, snow white, lamp black, pumpkin, green mist, country blue, heritage brick, forest green

Water-base varnish, matte finish

Tracing paper

Pencil

Graphite paper (light and dark)

Stylus

Paintbrushes: #2 flat, ½-inch flat, ⅜-inch angle, 10/0 liner

1. Prepare wood plate. If necessary, sand and then use tack cloth to remove dust. Mix equal amounts of deep midnight blue paint and water-base varnish; base and seal plate. Paint a second coat with deep midnight blue paint only. Let dry.

2. Trace or photocopy patterns on page 16. With large snowman pattern, light graphite paper, and stylus, transfer basic shapes of pattern onto plate. Base snowman with snow white. (This will take a few thin coats. Let dry between coats.) Base hat and coal with lamp black. Base carrot nose with pumpkin. Base scarf with green mist. Let dry.

3. Transfer details of pattern using dark graphite paper. With angle brush, float shade colors as follows: snow=country blue; carrot nose=heritage brick; scarf=forest green; hat and coal=country blue.

4. With liner brush, line carrot nose with heritage brick. Add highlights on coal eyes with snow white.

5. On plate rim, alternate pattern placement for little snowmen and snowflakes. Base coat snowmen with snow white and hats with lamp black. Let dry. With stylus, dot eyes, nose, and buttons on snowmen with lamp black. Line snowflakes with snow white and liner brush, and dot line ends with stylus and snow white. Let dry.

6. Finish with a coat of water-base varnish.

Snowman Crafts ❋ 15

Patterns are 100%.

A GAGGLE OF
Snow People Pins

Why decorate your coat with only one pin when you can have an amusing group of great snow people?!

What You'll Need
Tracing paper
Pencil
1 sheet clear shrink plastic
Scissors
Sandpaper (#230 to #320)
#03 black permanent marker
Acrylic paint: white, purple, midnight blue
#3 watercolor paintbrush
Permanent felt markers: carmine red, green, yellow, crimson red
Nonstick cookie sheet
Spatula
Clear gloss acrylic spray
3 adhesive pin backings

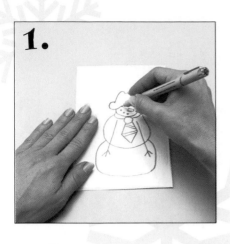

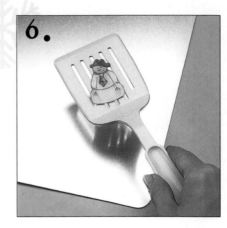

1. Photocopy or trace patterns on page 19. Cut a piece of plastic slightly larger than each pattern. Use sandpaper to roughen 1 side of plastic by sanding lightly in 1 direction; this will make paint adhere.

2. Place a piece of plastic over a pattern. Use #03 black marker to outline the snow person on plastic. Remove pattern. Repeat for all patterns.

3. Thin white paint with water to a wash consistency, and paint a thin coat on snow people's bodies. Let dry. Thin purple and midnight blue paints to wash consistency with water, and paint tall hat midnight blue and shorter hat purple. Let dry.

4. Use felt markers to color in noses, scarves, tie, purse, and hat brim of tall hat. (See finished picture for color placement.) Stroke colors on, avoiding overlapping strokes. Add details with black marker, and touch up outline if necessary.

5. Cut out snow people.

6. Bake on cookie sheet in 250-degree oven, painted side up. Snow people will shrink in 3 to 5 minutes. Wait until piece is about nickel thickness, then remove from oven. Use a spatula to remove from tray, and hold flat on spatula until cool (several seconds).

7. Spray the front (painted side) of each snow person with clear acrylic spray. Let dry for a few hours.

8. Remove adhesive from pin backings, and stick 1 to back of each snow person.

Patterns are 100%.

COUNTRY CUTE
Snow Paper

Your gift will look even better—and even more filled with love—
when you make your own paper to cover it!

What You'll Need
Tracing paper

Pencil

Scissors

Black marker

Sponges

Paper towels

Brown paper

Paper plates

Acrylic paint: white, black, brown, orange, red, green

Ball-head pin

Large, stiff-bristled paintbrush; old toothbrush; or Kemper tool

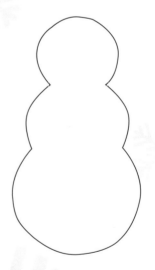

1. Enlarge and photo-copy or trace patterns below right, and cut them out. Trace patterns onto sponges with black marker, and cut out shapes. Run sponges under water, and press out excess water with paper towels.

2. Cut brown paper to size you need. Pour white paint onto a paper plate. Dip snowman sponge into paint, coating 1 side.

3. Sponge snowmen over the brown paper, pressing sponge onto paper. When sponge runs out of paint, reapply paint. Let snowmen dry.

4. Use black paint and sponge hat cutout to sponge hats on each snowman's head.

5. Use brown paint and twig cutout to sponge arms to sides of each snowman's body. Use orange paint and nose cutout to sponge a carrot nose on each snowman.

6. To make facial features, dip end of ball-head pin into black paint and dot on eyes and mouth. Use end of paintbrush to dot buttons on each snowman. Give half the snowmen red buttons using ball-headed pin, and give the other half green. Let dry completely.

7. Spatter-paint paper with white paint. To use a Kemper tool, fill bristles with white paint, hold brush over paper, and twist handle. Or, load paintbrush (or toothbrush) with white paint. Hold brush over paper, and run your finger over bristles. Let dry.

Enlarge patterns 200%.

Snowman Crafts ❄ 21

HEAVENLY Door Hanger

This heavenly snow person hangs on a doorknob and will make you smile each time you enter the room!

What You'll Need

Tracing paper

Pencil

Scissors

18×9-inch piece white velour knit

Straight pins

Sewing machine

White thread

Fiberfill

Needle

Quilting thread: white, black

2 black beads, 4mm each

2 black seed beads

12 inches gold cord, ¼ inch wide

Gold chenille stem

Glue gun, glue sticks

Clear plastic lid (such as a margarine lid)

Grease pencil

Gold glitter dimensional fabric paint

Silver fabric star

Small wreath, 1 inch diameter

Wooden skewer

Orange felt marker

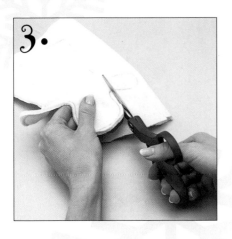

1. Enlarge and trace or photocopy patterns on page 25, and cut them out. Fold fabric in half widthwise, with right sides together. Pin snowman pattern to fabric, and trace around pattern with pencil.

2. Remove pattern, and pin layers of fabric together in several places. Thread sewing machine with white thread, and machine stitch along drawn line, leaving 2 inches open at the center bottom for turning.

3. With scissors, trim excess fabric from edge of stitching. Clip curves and corners.

4. Turn right side out through opening at bottom. Stuff figure with fiberfill through opening. Blind stitch opening closed with needle and white thread.

5. Wrap 18 inches of white quilting thread 3 times around neck of snow angel to form head. Tie a double knot to secure. Cut off excess thread.

6. Thread needle with doubled length of white thread, and stitch leg division, stitching through front and back of body. Fold arms to front, and stitch ends of hands together.

7. Use black quilting thread to sew on 4mm beads for eyes and to stitch eyebrows. Hide beginning and finishing knots under eye beads.

8. Begin mouth by stitching on a seed bead. Backstitch mouth, finishing with a seed bead at opposite end. Tie gold cord around neck in a bow.

9. Bend an end of gold chenille stem into a 1-inch-diameter circle, twisting end back around itself. Glue remaining portion of chenille stem down center of angel's back. (Trim end of chenille stem if it is too long.)

10. Trace around wing pattern on plastic lid with grease pencil. Cut out wings. Outline edge of wings with dimensional glitter paint; let 1 side dry thoroughly before painting other side. Let wings dry for several hours before attaching.

11. Attach wings to angel's back with needle and white quilting thread, making several cross-stitches over center of wings. Glue silver star to center of wings, covering stitches. Stitch wreath to angel's hands with white quilting thread.

12. Cut end off wooden skewer, and paint tip orange with marker. Glue tip to center of face for nose. Thread a loop of quilting thread to top of head for a hanger; knot ends together.

Enlarge patterns 125%.

WARM AND WONDERFUL
Welcome Mat

Despite its winter scene, this mat will warm the "soles" of your guests as they step inside your home! What better way to make someone feel welcome than with a friendly snow family!

What You'll Need
Tracing paper

Pencil

Scissors

Poster board or cardboard

Stylus

Graphite paper

Craft knife

Rug (short pile, solid dark color)

White chalk

Small stencil brush

Acrylic paint: snow white, forest green, lamp black, green mist, slate grey, milk chocolate, moon yellow, country blue

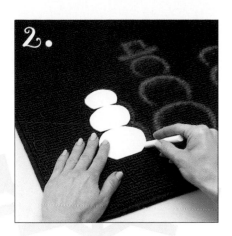

1. Trace or photocopy the patterns on page 28; each circle template must be a separate shape. Cut out circles, and trace them onto cardboard. Cut them out. Trace remaining patterns on cardboard with stylus and graphite paper. Use a craft knife to cut out insides of patterns, creating stencils.

2. Determine the number of snow people you'd like on your mat; you can make the same number as you have family members. Begin placing the bottom sections of each snow person onto rug, and trace around templates with chalk. See chart at right for circle placement. Once you are happy with placement, continue placing upper body sections and tracing around them with chalk.

3. Place tree stencils in background, and line shapes with chalk. Chalk in hat and broom stencils. Create a ground line with snow white paint, leaving a small space under the base of the snow people.

4. With stencil brush, dab snow white to snow people's bodies, applying paint more heavily on top of each section. (This will require more than 1 coat of paint.) Apply forest green to tree sections, applying paint more heavily at the bottom of branches. Apply lamp black to hat. Let dry.

5. With green mist, highlight the tips of tree branches. With slate grey, highlight hat edges. Apply lamp black for coal on snow people's faces and buttons. On broom handle use milk chocolate, and on broom bristles use moon yellow.

6. Line WELCOME with country blue. Let dry.

	TOP	MIDDLE	BOTTOM
Man	2	4	5
Woman*	2	4	5
Teen	1	2	3
Child**	1	2	3

* (Make woman slightly shorter than man.)
**(Make child slightly shorter than teen.)

5
4
3
2
1

WELCOME

*Enlarge "Welcome" 300%;
all other patterns are 100%.*

CAPTIVATING
Centerpiece

With these three snowmen adorning your holiday table, your dinner parties are sure to be a hit!

What You'll Need

Newspaper

3 clay pots: one 5 inch, two 3 inch

Foam balls: one 4 inch, three 2½ inch, two 2 inch

7 craft sticks

Glue gun, glue sticks

Paint-on snow

Spanish moss

Orange oven-bake polymer clay

Epoxy

6 black screw-on doll eyes, 6mm each

Black acrylic paint

Paintbrush

Black felt hats: one 3 inch, two 2½ inch

6 silk poinsettias: three 2 inch, three 4 inch

6½ yards plaid wired ribbon

Scissors

Blue fleece fabric

4 silk pinecone and evergreen sprigs, 4 inches each

1. Crunch up newspaper, and fill large clay pot half full. Place 4-inch foam ball in clay pot for position; ball should sit half in and half out of pot. If needed, add more newspaper. Take ball out of pot, and poke a craft stick in the center of newspapers. Glue stick in place.

2. Push 4-inch ball on craft stick. Insert another craft stick in top center of foam ball. Push 2½-inch ball on craft stick to form snowman.

3. Repeat steps 1 and 2 with small pots and remaining foam balls; 2½-inch balls are lower bodies and 2-inch balls are heads.

4. With a craft stick, apply paint-on snow to all 3 snowmen. Let paint dry for 24 hours.

5. When snow is completely dry, hot glue Spanish moss around edges of clay pots, filling in around snowmen.

6. Roll ½-inch ball of orange clay into a carrot nose. Make 2 slightly smaller noses for small snowmen. Bake following manufacturer's directions. Glue to faces using epoxy.

7. With end of a paintbrush, dot mouths using black paint. Let dry. Insert eyes into faces.

8. Place large hat on big snowman and small hats on other snowmen. Glue in place with glue gun. Glue a small clump of Spanish moss to each hat, and glue a 2-inch poinsettia in center of moss.

9. Measure and cut ribbon to fit around top edge of each pot. Glue in place. For large pot, make a bow with eight 4-inch loops. Cut a 10-inch piece of ribbon, and cut ends at an angle. Fold ribbon in half to make a V. Glue folded end to center front of large clay pot. Fluff bow, and glue it on top of folded end of tails. For smaller pots, make bows with eight 3-inch loops, and cut an 8-inch length for tails.

10. Cut a 1¾×24-inch length and two 1½×24-inch lengths from the blue fleece for scarves. Tie the larger scarf around the biggest snowman. Tie the smaller scarves around the necks of the smaller snowmen.

11. For large clay pot, insert and hot glue a 4-inch poinsettia in front of snowman. Next to it and back to the side, insert and glue an evergreen sprig. Behind that glue another 4-inch poinsettia, and behind that an evergreen sprig.

12. For small pots, insert and glue a 4-inch poinsettia in front of snowman, and back to the side insert and glue an evergreen sprig.

SNOWY
Stationery

During those long winter months, when we're cooped up inside, it's important to keep in touch. What better way than with this cheerful stationery!

What You'll Need
White ink pad
Heavy paper: red, blue, yellow
Markers: black, orange, green, red, brown
White pen

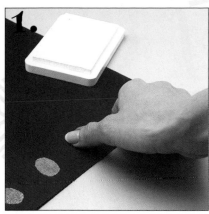

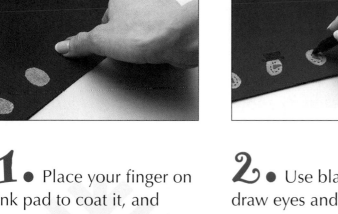

1. Place your finger on ink pad to coat it, and stamp finger on paper for snowman heads. Place heads in a pleasing arrangement. You could also stack 2 or 3 finger stamps to create the snowman bodies.

2. Use black marker to draw eyes and mouths. Use orange marker to draw carrot noses. You could also draw holly using green marker and add berries with red marker. If you are making standing snowmen, use brown marker to add arms. Use black marker to add hats where you want them. If you'd like, add halos with white pen to make snow angels.

3. Use white pen to write sayings on paper, such as "Let It Snow!" or "There's No People Like Snow People!"

A Mug of
WINTER WARMTH

What better way to warm up your brood of snowman builders than with hot chocolate in friendly snowman mugs!

What You'll Need

Tracing paper

Pencil

White ceramic mug

Scissors

Clear tape

Grease pencil

Enamel paint: black, orange, blue, green, red, white

Paintbrushes

Paper towel

2.

4.

6.

7.

1. Trace or photocopy the pattern below. Cut pattern out, and tape to side of cup.

2. Use grease pencil to trace around outside shape. Remove pattern.

3. From paper pattern, cut out hat and nose. Tape them on cup, and use grease pencil to trace around pieces. Cut out holly, and trace that on cup. Draw in eyes, mouth, and neckline of sweater.

4. Paint hat black, nose orange, and sweater blue. Let paint dry. Paint eyes, nose outline, mouth, and face outline with black. Let paint dry.

5. Paint holly green and berries red. Add white to blue paint to make light blue. Paint a light blue shadow under brim of hat and light blue vertical stripes on sweater.

6. Use same light blue paint to add snowflakes around mug.

7. Add enough water to red paint to make a wash, and paint a cheek on snowman.

8. Let paint dry thoroughly for several hours. Wipe off any grease pencil with damp paper towel. Cure paint according to directions on paint jars.

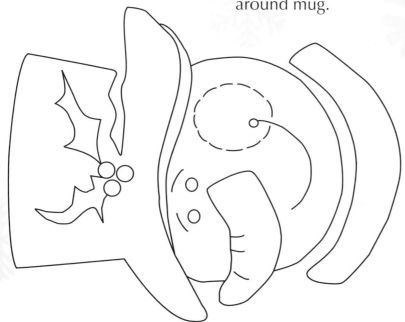

Pattern is 100%.

MARVELOUS
Mitten Hanging

This snowman mitten hanging will amuse everyone while decorating your wall with the wonder of winter!

What You'll Need

White paper

Pencil

³⁄₈-yard fuzzy felt

Straight pins

Scissors

5×3-inch orange felt

Scrap iron-on adhesive

Iron

Black embroidery floss

Embroidery needle

2 black buttons, ⁵⁄₈ inch each

Sewing machine

8×18 inches plaid fabric

Raffia

Safety pin

Silk and plastic greenery and holly

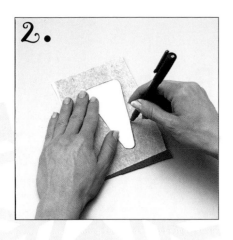

1. Photocopy or trace the patterns below, and cut them out. Pin mitten pattern to doubled felt fabric, and cut out.

2. Iron adhesive to back of orange felt; trace nose pattern onto paper. Cut out.

3. Iron nose to mitten front. With floss, stitch nose and mouth. Sew on button eyes.

4. With right sides facing, pin mitten front and back together. Sew ¼ inch seam. Clip corners. Turn inside out.

5. Fold plaid material lengthwise with right sides together; iron. Use a running stitch to sew short ends together to make a large loop. Place cuff inside mitten, with seam of cuff facing inside. Use a running stitch to sew cuff on, stitching ½ inch away from edge. Turn cuff to outside of mitten.

6. Tie a bow using raffia, and pin it to cuff with safety pin. Place greenery and holly inside mitten and arrange.

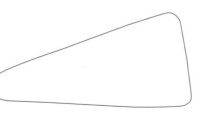

Enlarge patterns 200%.

DELIGHTFULLY BIRDY
Denim Shirt

Birds need shelter, especially in winter. This friendly snowman offers a bird a bevy of birdhouses from which to choose!

What You'll Need

Denim shirt

⅛ yard iron-on adhesive

Iron

6×7-inch white calico fabric

Calico cloth scraps: blue, yellow, light brown, dark brown, orange, black, red

White paper

Pencil

Scissors

Black paint

4 beige buttons

Fabric glue

Ball-headed pin

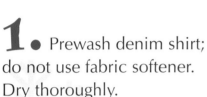

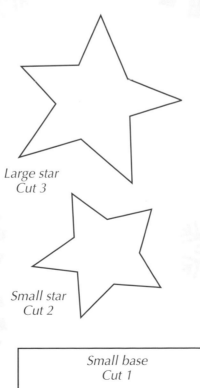

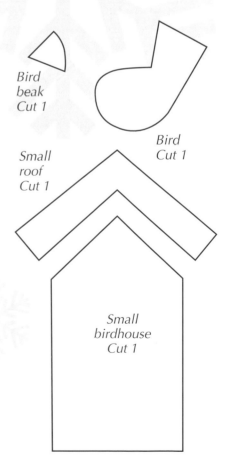

1. Prewash denim shirt; do not use fabric softener. Dry thoroughly.

2. Apply iron-on adhesive, using manufacturer's instruction, to the back of each fabric.

3. Photocopy or trace the patterns on this page and page 40, and cut them out. Trace patterns to paper backing on each fabric. Trace snowman, hands, and snow ledge on white; bird, jacket, small birdhouse, large roof, and large base on blue; beak, 3 large stars, and 2 small stars on yellow; large birdhouse and 1 hole on light brown; 2 holes, small roof, and small base on dark brown; nose on orange; hat on black; scarf on red fabric. Cut out all pieces.

4. Peel paper backing off each fabric piece. Place them on shirt according to finished photograph. Place snowman's hands under sleeves, and place hat on head. Place roofs and bases on top of birdhouses. Place holes on top of each birdhouse. Press in place.

5. Glue buttons to centers of stars (except star on pocket).

6. Use ball-headed pin and black paint to dot on smile and eyes of snowman.

Bird beak
Cut 1

Bird
Cut 1

Small roof
Cut 1

Large star
Cut 3

Small star
Cut 2

Small base
Cut 1

Small birdhouse
Cut 1

Patterns are 100%.

Snowman Crafts ❄ 39

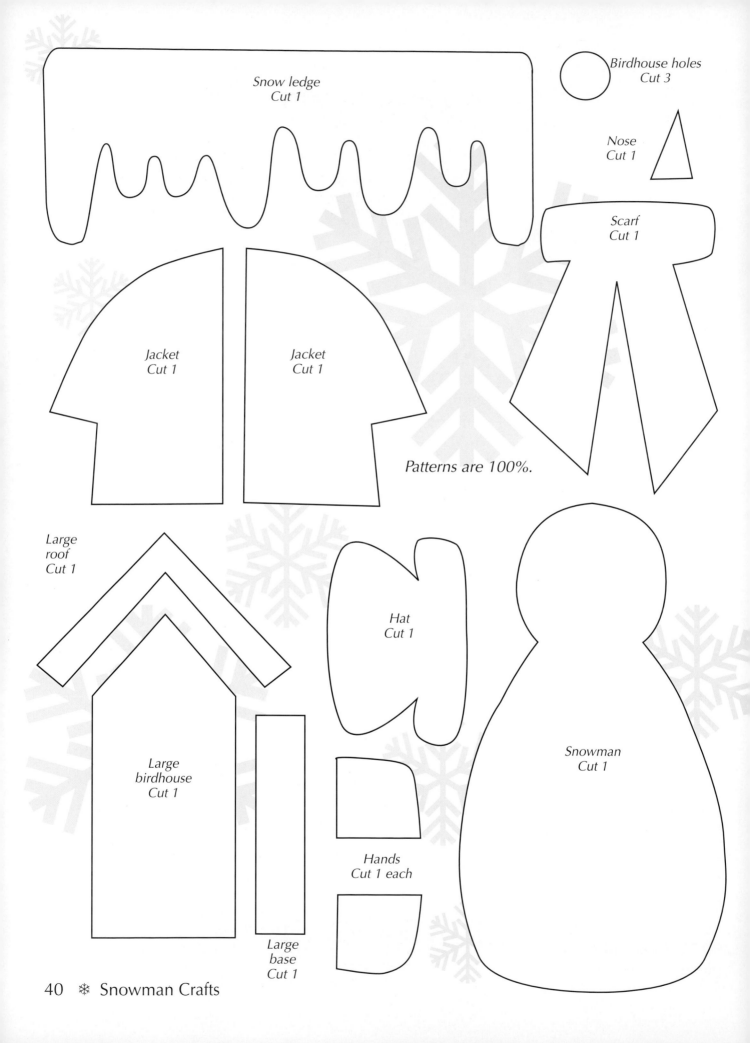

Snow ledge
Cut 1

Birdhouse holes
Cut 3

Nose
Cut 1

Scarf
Cut 1

Jacket
Cut 1

Jacket
Cut 1

Patterns are 100%.

Large
roof
Cut 1

Hat
Cut 1

Snowman
Cut 1

Large
birdhouse
Cut 1

Hands
Cut 1 each

Large
base
Cut 1

SNOW FAMILY
Wreath

This colorful holiday wreath features a delightful snow family to greet your guests.

What You'll Need

26-gauge craft wire

Scissors

24-inch green pine wreath

Tracing paper

Graphite paper

Pencil

$1/4$-inch board, 18×18-inch piece

Band- or jigsaw

Medium grade sandpaper

Acrylic paint: white, pink, black, orange, red, kelly green

Paintbrushes: flat, liner

White textural snow medium

Wood circles: five $3/8$ inch, two $3/4$ inch

2 wood hearts, $7/8$ inch each

Air-dry paper clay

Glue gun, glue sticks

15 black beads, $1/8$ inch each

$2\frac{1}{6}$ yards wire-edged plaid ribbon, $2\frac{1}{2}$ inches wide

Fabric stiffener

Clothespins

Ruler

1 yard red cord, $1/4$ inch wide

Fray check

8 red pompoms, 1 inch each

2 yards each red and green ribbon, $1/16$ inch wide

4-inch natural straw hat

5 to 7 red silk flowers, about $3/4$ inch each

Red berries: five to seven $1/2$ to $3/4$ inch, nine 1 inch

Green florist tape

3 inches red satin ribbon, $3/8$ inch wide

2 screw eyes, $1/4$ inch each

4-inch black top hat

6 pinecones, $1\frac{1}{2}$ to $2\frac{1}{2}$ inches

1. To make a hanger, cut a length of wire about 8 inches long. Twist wire around wire form on back of wreath to make a loop. Set aside.

2. Trace or photocopy the patterns on page 44. Transfer patterns to board with graphite paper, and cut out snow family and 6 mittens. Sand.

3. Paint snow family white. Let dry. Apply second coat. Let dry. Apply coat of snow medium over white paint. Let dry.

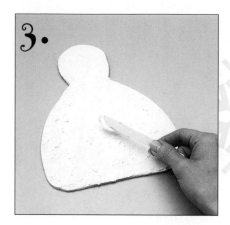

4. Cut a ³⁄₄-inch circle and a ⁷⁄₈-inch heart in half for cheeks. Discard half of each. Paint halves and other ³⁄₄-inch circle pink. Let dry.

5. Cut a ³⁄₈-inch circle in half. Paint the half circles and the remaining ³⁄₈-inch circles black. Let dry. These are eyes.

6. From the paper clay, make two 1-inch noses and one ³⁄₄-inch nose. Make the 1-inch noses bend slightly. Air-dry clay. Paint orange, and let dry.

7. Assemble the snow family. Glue cheeks, half cheeks, noses, and eyes into place. Glue on beads for mouths. (See photo for placement.)

8. Cut 6 inches of wired ribbon, and apply fabric stiffener. Let dry. Cut into a tie shape, and glue around pop's neck. Hold with clothespins until dry.

9. Paint 4 mittens red and 2 mittens kelly green. Let dry. Apply second coat. Let dry. Paint 2 red mittens with a plaid design. With ruler and pencil, draw

straight lines horizontally 1-inch apart, then draw vertical lines 1-inch apart. Cover pencil lines with black paint. Let dry. Paint a thin green line next to black lines.

10. Cut ¹⁄₄-inch cord into three 12-inch pieces. Tie a knot on both ends of each piece, and seal end with Fray check. Glue an end of cord to back of thumb side of a mitten and other end of cord to matching mitten. Glue a pompom on each mitten, in front of where cord is glued. Set aside.

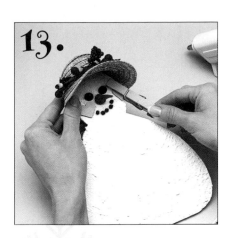

11. Tie 2 yards of 2½-inch ribbon into a 5-inch bow with 5 loops. Leave a 16-inch and a 6-inch tail. With thin craft wire, attach bow to upper right side of wreath; place long tail at wreath top. Make a loop in long tail and secure to wreath with wire.

12. Make a 1-inch multiloop bow from both colors of ¹⁄₁₆-inch ribbon. With thin wire, attach bow around snowmom's neck. Cover wire with ribbon. Attach snowmom to left side of wreath with thin craft wire. Move pine pieces under mom so she sticks out from wreath.

13. Split back of straw hat. Use florist tape to assemble a few flowers and berries into a bouquet. Glue bouquet above front rim of hat. Overlap back of hat on snowmom's head so it fits snugly, and glue in place. If necessary, hold with clothespins until dry.

14. Glue ³⁄₈-inch satin ribbon over top of junior's head. Glue remaining pompoms to each end of ribbon to form earmuffs. To attach junior, screw eyes on both sides of junior's body. Twist 1 end of wire around a screw eye, and run wire around wreath's back and up to second screw eye. Twist wire around second screw eye, and trim ends. Bend pine pieces under his body so he sticks out some from body of wreath.

15. Glue pop's hat on his head. Wire snow-pop to bottom right side of wreath.

16. Attach wires to mittens; place plaid mittens at top center, green mittens under bow, and red mittens to bottom left side of wreath.

17. Wire 2 pinecones and 3 berries together in a cluster. Make 3 clusters. Attach clusters to wreath in a pleasing manner.

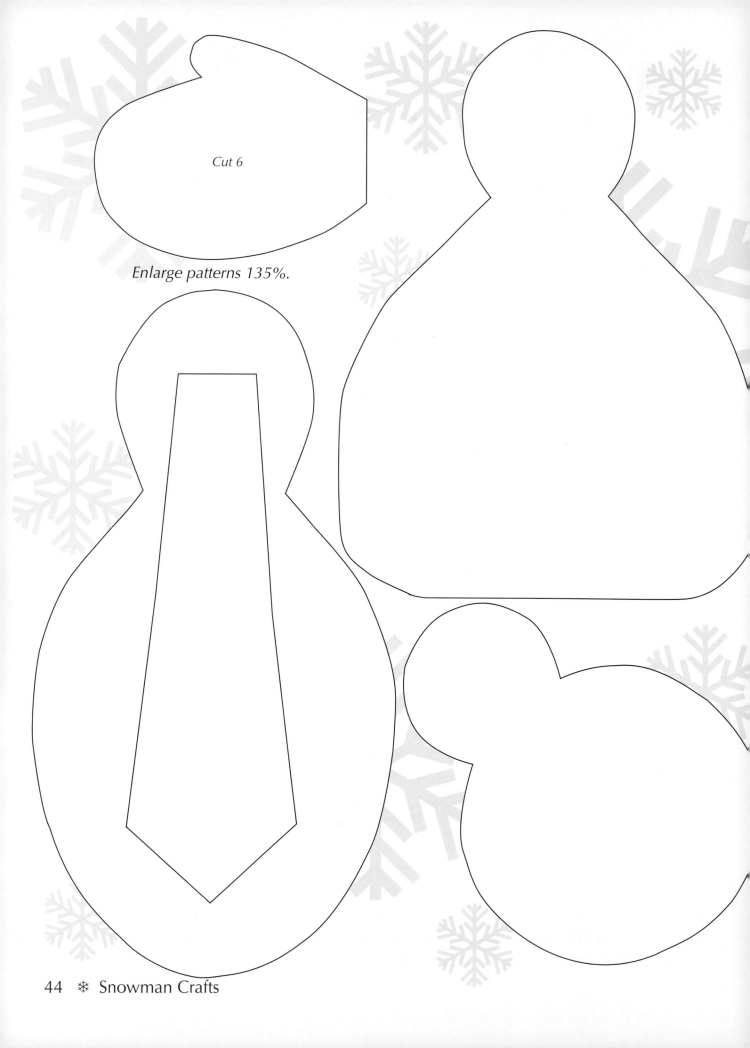

Cut 6

Enlarge patterns 135%.

JOLLY HOLLY SNOWMAN
Ornament

This happy guy is just hanging around, bringing warmth and cheer during the long days of winter!

What You'll Need

12×12-inch lightweight batting

Scissors

4-inch foam ball

Embroidery needle

Black embroidery floss

Pencil

12 inches black ribbon, ³⁄₈ inch wide

Hot glue gun, glue sticks

3-inch felt hat

Craft knife

Tracing paper

3×3-inch orange felt scrap

Orange thread, needle

2 black doll eyes, 6mm each

Powder blush

Cotton swab

Spanish moss

3-inch sprig silk holly

Blue calico fabric scrap

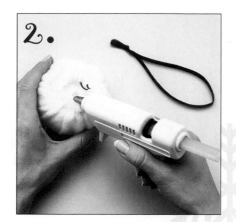

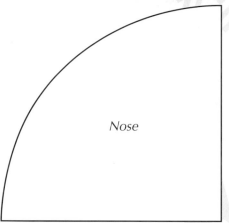

1. Cut a circle of batting to almost cover foam ball—there should be a little of top of foam ball uncovered. (Reserve batting scraps.) Cut an 18-inch length of floss; pull out 1 strand. Thread needle with floss strand, and sew a running stitch around edge of batting circle for gathering. Place foam ball on center of batting, and pull thread so batting covers ball. Knot thread.

2. Use end of pencil to poke a small hole in top of foam ball. Fold black ribbon in half, and tie ends in a knot to make a loop. Hot glue ribbon knot into hole of foam ball. Hold until glue sets.

3. Lightly stuff hat with batting scraps. Use craft knife to cut a small slit in top of hat, then insert rib-

Nose

Pattern is 100%.

bon loop coming up from bottom of hat through top. Glue hat to top of foam ball.

4. Trace nose pattern on orange felt. Cut out, and stitch straight edges together. Trim seam allowance, and turn nose to right side. Stuff nose lightly with batting scraps. Hot glue nose to face. (Be sure seam faces down.)

5. With craft knife, make small slits in face where eyes will be. Insert eyes into foam ball.

6. Using 6 strands of floss, stitch a smile on face, knotting at each end of smile. Use cotton swab and powder blush to make cheeks.

7. Glue Spanish moss and holly to hat. Tear a 2½×18-inch strip from blue calico, and tie a bow with 2-inch tails. Cut bow ends on a diagonal, and glue bow to bottom of snowman's head.

A LOVELY
ASSORTMENT OF
Snow People Garland

These happy snow people will bring a smile to your face every time you catch a glimpse of them!

What You'll Need

Tracing paper
Pencil
Temporary spray adhesive
5-inch length of wood (such as poplar or basswood), 8 inches wide and ½ inch thick
⅛-inch drill bit, 5 inches in length
#2 reverse tooth scroll saw blades
Scroll saw
Medium and fine grade sandpaper
Tack cloth

Acrylic paints: buttercream, Prussian blue, white, fiesta pink, bittersweet orange, crocus yellow, tangerine, burnt umber, black, heritage green, mallard green, chamomile, light Victorian teal, pthalo green, mocha brown, rhythm 'n blue, touch 'o pink, Bahama purple, royal fuchsia, sweetheart blush, purple, pale lilac, drizzle grey, napthol crimson, tompte red, periwinkle blue, coastline blue, pthalo blue, pink

quartz, pink silk, ocean reef blue, sparkle glaze
Paintbrushes: various sizes of flat, angled-shaders, liners; stippler
Stylus
Interior/exterior varnish
16 round wood beads, ½ inch each
28 round wood beads, ⅜ inch each
Two ⅛-inch dowel rods, approximately 12 inches long each
2 yards hemp cord

 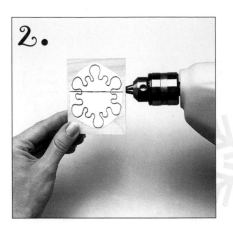 

1. Photocopy or trace patterns on page 51. Apply temporary spray adhesive to backs of patterns, and apply them to wood in direction of the grain. Rough cut pieces apart into blocks, being sure that side edges are perpendicular to dotted lines.

2. With the ⅛-inch drill bit, carefully drill through where dotted line indicates. (You may want to practice on wood scraps to get the feel of going through wood without breaking sides.) Be sure to stay in center of each piece so bit doesn't "blow out" sides. Don't force bit through the wood; let the bit do the work.

3. After drilling all holes, cut around perimeter of all pieces with #2 reverse tooth blade of scroll saw. Lightly sand pieces, and use tack cloth to remove dust.

4. General painting instructions for all snowpeople: When painting base colors, continue painting around sides of all pieces. Base coat bodies, heads, and faces with buttercream. Paint all clothing, hats, and carried items according to individual instructions. (Specific painting instructions for each snow person follow.) Float shade around all buttercream areas (including sides) with Prussian blue.

5. Use stippler brush to stipple over body and head with white. Keep stippling light and airy, and allow floated shades to show through. Stipple sides of snow people in same manner.

6. Dry-brush cheeks with a very light hint of fiesta pink, building color. Base coat nose with bittersweet orange. Float a line of crocus yellow on top third of nose. Float a shade on underside of nose with tangerine. With liner brush, make a tiny line of burnt umber on underside of nose.

7. With small side of stylus and black paint, dot eyes. Line mouth and eyebrows with black. With stylus and white paint, add a highlight in each eye.

8. Snowman with star: Base coat star with crocus yellow. Base coat mittens, hat band, and pompom with heritage green. Base coat scarf and hat with mallard green.

9. Dry-brush center area of star with chamomile. Dry-brush green areas very lightly with light Victorian teal to highlight.

10. Paint stripes on scarf with heritage green. Float shade on all green areas with pthalo green. Float shade on star with mocha brown.

11. Snowwoman with baby: Base coat hat, cape, and mittens with rhythm 'n blue. Base coat baby blanket, hatband, and bow with touch 'o pink. Dry brush center areas of cape with Bahama purple.

12. Float shade on blanket, hatband, and bow with royal fuchsia. Refloat blanket, hatband, and bow with sweetheart blush to strengthen. Float shade on hat, cape, and mittens with purple. Dry-brush purple areas with pale lilac.

13. Base coat hat flower with crocus yellow. Float shade with mocha brown. Dot center of flower with crocus yellow.

14. Snowman with broom: Base coat hat with drizzle grey. Base coat scarf and mittens with napthol crimson. Base coat hatband and broom with crocus yellow. Base coat broom handle with mocha brown.

15. Float shade on hat band with napthol crimson. Float shade on broom with mocha brown. Float shade on bristles and broom handle with burnt umber.

16. Dry-brush mittens and center area of scarf with bittersweet orange. Paint lines on scarf with crocus yellow. Float shade on scarf and mittens with tompte red. Float shade on hat with black. Dry brush top and sides of hat with black.

17. Snowman with shovel: Base coat hatband, pompom, and scarf with crocus yellow. Base coat hat and mittens with bittersweet orange. Base coat shovel with drizzle grey. Base coat shovel handle with mocha brown.

18. Float shade on hat, scarf, and mittens with tangerine. Strengthen floats with mocha brown. Float shade on shovel with black. Float shade on shovel handle with burnt umber.

19. Snowman with birdhouse: Base coat hat and scarf with periwinkle blue. Base coat hatband, pompom, and mittens with coastline blue. Base coat birdhouse with chamomile. Base coat roof and birdhouse pole with mocha brown.

20. Float shade on hat and scarf with pthalo blue. Float shade on birdhouse with mocha brown. Float shade on roof and birdhouse pole with burnt umber. Use large end of stylus and black paint to dot hole on birdhouse.

21. Snowwoman with basket: Base coat hat, hat bow, mittens, apron, and apron bow with pink quartz. Base coat the ruffles on hat and apron with touch 'o pink. Base coat basket with crocus yellow.

22. Dry brush top of hat, center of mittens, and apron with pink silk. Dry brush hat and apron ruffles lightly in center with white.

23. Float shade on hat, mittens, apron, and bows with royal fuchsia. Float shade on basket with mocha brown. Strengthen floats on hat, apron, and mittens with sweetheart blush. Float shade on inside of basket with burnt umber. Lightly strengthen floats on basket and do linework with burnt umber.

24. Snowflakes: Base coat snowflakes with buttercream. Stipple (including sides) with white, allowing buttercream to show through. Float shade with ocean reef blue. Stipple sides of snowflakes lightly with ocean reef blue. Lightly paint, including sides, with sparkle glaze.

25. After each piece is finished, apply several coats of varnish. Let dry between coats.

26. Garland beads: After stringing small beads on a dowel, paint them white. After stringing larger beads on other dowel, paint them ocean reef blue. When dry, apply several coats of varnish while beads are still on dowels. Remove when varnish is dry.

27. Finishing: Tie a blue bead to the end of the hemp cord. First string on a white bead, then a blue bead, a white bead, a snowflake, a white bead, a blue bead, a white bead, and a snow person. Repeat process, stringing on remaining beads, snowflakes, and snow people. Finish by tying on remaining blue bead to end of hemp. The finished garland is about 32 inches long.

Cut 7

Patterns are 100%.

TOP HAT,
the Ring Toss
Snowman

This easy craft is a perfect project to do with your kids. You all get some quality time, and they end up with a great toy!

What You'll Need

Small round wood finial, about 1⅜ inches

Medium grade sandpaper

Hammer

¾-inch brad

12-inch dowel rod, ⅜ inch diameter

Wire cutter

Awl

Wood glue

Glue gun, glue sticks

Large wood bead, with ⅜-inch opening

Acrylic paint: white, light foliage green, purple, black, orange

Paintbrush

Empty jar

2-inch wood curtain ring

Waxed paper

Clear gloss acrylic spray

Small plastic hat

2 small screw eyes

#3 perle floss, 15 inches

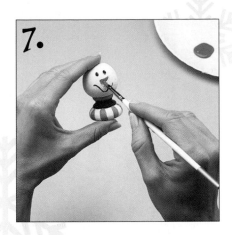

1. Sand rough edges of finial. (If finial has a knob, remove with a saw.)

2. Use hammer to pound brad into center of 1 end of dowel. With wire cutter, cut off brad head.

3. Use awl to punch small hole into center bottom of finial. Push brad in dowel into hole of finial. Add a drop of wood glue to secure nail in hole. Let dry 30 minutes.

4. Hot glue wood bead to other end of dowel.

5. Paint finial white. Let dry. Paint a band with light foliage green on ridge below large bulb, and paint a purple band on ridge below green band. On last ridge, paint green vertical stripes. Paint underside of finial green,

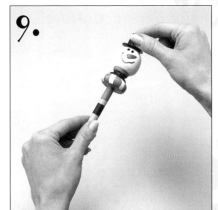

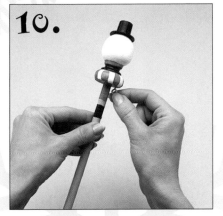

and add a wide green stripe on dowel below finial. Leave ¼ inch of dowel below green stripe unpainted, and paint a wide purple stripe. Stand dowel in jar to dry.

6. Paint bead at end of dowel green. Stand dowel in jar, bead side up, and let dry. Paint curtain ring green, and let dry on waxed paper.

7. Paint eyes and mouth black and nose orange. Let dry. Outline carrot nose with black.

8. Stand dowel in jar, and spray finial with gloss spray. Place curtain ring on waxed paper, and spray. Let dry. Turn dowel upside down, and spray bead. Turn ring over, and spray. Let dry.

9. Hot glue plastic hat to top of head.

10. Screw eye to underside of finial; screw other eye to curtain ring. Tie 1 end of perle floss to eye in ring and other end of floss to eye on finial.

SENSATIONAL
Spiral Ornament

*This snowy spring of a snowman is fun to make, and
he'll add some bounce to your holiday decorating!*

What You'll Need

White paper

Pencil

5-inch square white
card stock

Clear tape

Scissors

Black fine-point felt pen

Orange felt pen

4-inch square black
construction paper

1-inch square each of red
and green paper

Craft glue

1/8-inch hole punch

8 inches cord

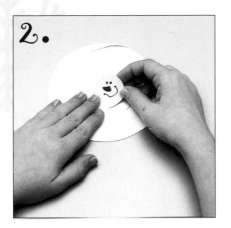

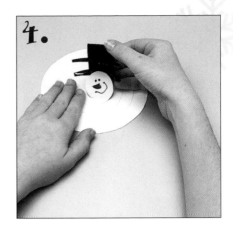

1. Enlarge the patterns below. Tape the spiral pattern to the card stock, and cut out following the lines on the pattern. Remove the pattern.

2. Draw the eyes, nose, and mouth on the head—the center of the spiral—using the black felt pen. Color the nose orange. Fold the head upward.

Enlarge patterns 200%.

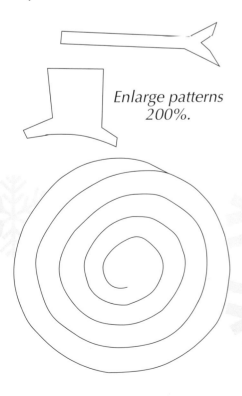

3. Cut out the patterns for the arm and the hat. Trace around arm pattern twice on the black paper, and cut out. Fold the remaining piece of black paper in half, and place top edge of the hat pattern along the fold. Trace around the pattern, and cut it out. (Don't cut fold.)

4. Apply glue to the inside of the hat, and slip it over the snowman's head. Press the hat pieces together, sandwiching the head between. Glue an arm to each side of the first spiral below the head.

5. From the green paper, cut out 2 holly leaves. Use the hole punch to make a red berry from the red paper. Glue the holly leaves and the berry to the hat.

6. Punch a hole in the center top of the hat. Fold the cord in half, tie the ends of the cord together. Push the cord loop through the hole, and thread the tied ends of cord through the protruding loop of the cord. Hang your spiral friend wherever you'd like!

Jumping Jack
SNOWMAN

*Dance, Jack, dance! This happy guy will keep you laughing and having fun—
staying in the house this winter is going to be a blast!*

What You'll Need

Tracing paper

Pencil

15×10-inch white mat board

Heavy-duty scissors

Permanent felt markers:
black, violet, aqua, yellow,
gold, red

Dimensional fabric paint:
silver glitter, slick black

Newspaper

Awl

Hammer

Heavy-duty needle

4 brass paper fasteners with
¼-inch shank

Carpet or upholstery thread

Craft glue

12 inches #3 perle cotton
floss

1 medium purple bead

1. Photocopy or trace the patterns from page 59, and cut them out. Trace around the patterns on the mat board with the pencil. (For arms and legs, trace around pattern once, turn pattern over, and trace around pattern a second time.) Cut out all the pieces from the mat board. To cut inside curves and corners, make little cuts into the edges of the curve or corner, then go back and cut along drawn line.

2. With the black marker, go over all the edges to create outlines. Look at the pattern to sketch in the details (the right knee patch, the scarf, the facial features, etc.) with the pencil. Go over the pencil lines with the black marker.

3. Color the hat, gloves, scarf, patch, and skates with the felt markers, using the finished photo as a guide for colors. With the silver glitter dimensional paint, outline the blades of the ice skates. With the slick black paint, outline the stripes on the hat and the scarf and the stitches on the patch. Use the black paint to outline the buttons and make dots for the eyes and mouth. Let paint dry completely.

4. Place the cut-out pieces on a thick pad of newspaper. With the awl and hammer, punch large holes where shown on all the pattern pieces. Make sure holes are large enough for the end of a brass fastener to slide into. Use the heavy-duty needle to make small holes in all 4 limbs where shown on the pattern pieces.

5. Cut a 6-inch piece of carpet thread, and thread the heavy-duty needle. Push the needle through the small hole of 1 arm, and tie the end of the thread around the end of the arm with a double knot. Attach the arm to the backside of the body with a brass fastener. Bend back the ends of the fastener just enough to allow the arm to swing freely.

6. Push the carpet thread through the small hole on the other arm, and attach the arm to the body with a brass fastener. Pull the thread taut, and knot it around the end of the arm with a double knot. Cut off excess thread. Add a small dot of glue to each knot. Let dry.

7. Follow steps 5 and 6 to attach the legs.

8. Tie an end of the perle cotton floss to the center of the carpet thread that connects the arms. Bring floss down to the thread connecting the legs, and knot the floss on that thread, leaving a tail of floss hanging.

9. Tie the bead to the end of the floss. Test Jack by pulling on the bead—he should jump and dance. If necessary, adjust how tight or loose the brass fasteners are so he can really boogie!

Patterns are 100%.

Cut 2

Cut 2

SIMPLY SUPERB
Snowman Magnet

This guy is fun to make, and he'll stick around to help you hang up your school notes and pictures, or even to show off your great report card!

What You'll Need

Tracing paper

Pencil

Scissors

2mm foam sheets: white, turquoise, brown, orange, black

Craft glue

2 wiggle eyes, 7mm each

3 black buttons, $7/16$ inch each

$5\frac{1}{2}$ inches adhesive magnet strip

1. Photocopy or trace the patterns below, and cut them out.

2. Using the patterns, trace the shapes on the following colors of foam: snowman on white, scarf on turquoise, twig arms on brown (make 2), carrot nose on orange, and hat on black. Cut pieces out.

3. With the craft glue, attach the hat to the snowman's head, the scarf around his neck, the twig arms on both sides of his upper body, and the nose to the middle of his face. Glue the wiggle eyes above the nose, and glue the buttons down the center of his body.

4. Peel the backing from the magnet strip, and lay the magnet down the back of the snowman. Now he's ready to work for you, hanging around and holding your notes and important papers!

Patterns are 100%.

SNOW BUDDY
Pencil Topper

*This pencil topper is sure to be the envy of all your friends—
so why not make one for each of them
this holiday season!*

What You'll Need
Air-dry paper clay
Pencil
Round wood toothpicks
Acrylic paint: black, green,
red, orange
Small paintbrush
Ball-headed pin
Craft glue
10 black beads, $^{11}/_0$ each
Scrap blue felt
Scissors

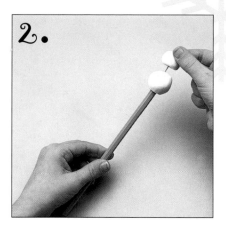

1. To make the body of the snowman, roll a 1-inch ball of clay. Insert the end of the pencil halfway into the body. Break a wood toothpick in half, and insert half of it into the center top of the body.

2. Make the head by rolling a ⁷/₈-inch ball of clay. Place this on the top of the body. Slightly flatten the top of the head.

3. To make the hat, flatten a ⁵/₈-inch ball of clay into a 1¹/₈-inch circle. Roll a ⁷/₈-inch ball, and slightly flatten the top and bottom of it (the sides should stay rounded). Place the flattened ball on the brim to complete the hat.

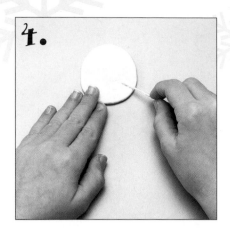  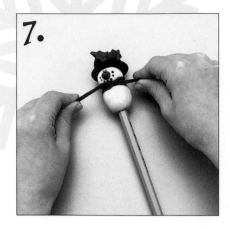

4. Flatten a 2-inch ball of clay, and cut out 2 holly leaves with a toothpick. Make lines in the center of the leaves with the end of the toothpick. Roll a $\frac{1}{8}$-inch ball into a carrot shape. Let the body, hat, leaves, small ball, and carrot shape all dry for 24 hours.

5. When the pieces have dried, paint the hat black, the holly leaves green, the small ball red, and the carrot nose orange. Use the ball-head of the pin and the black paint to dot eyes and a mouth on the snowman's face. Let paint dry completely.

6. Glue the holly leaves and red ball to the top of the snowman's hat. Glue the hat to the top of the snowman's head, and glue the carrot nose to the snowman's face.

7. Cut a $\frac{1}{4} \times 10$-inch piece of blue felt. Tie it around the snowman's neck, and glue the ends down. With your snow buddy's help, your homework is sure to get done even quicker!